THEATRE LEISURE NEEDS FACTORS

JOHN LOK

Copyright © John Lok
All Rights Reserved.

Contents

Preface

Introduction

Any theatre performance must need have good seats and hall facilities to let audiences to feel comfortable to see any performances, instead of facilities supply requirement. Audiences visual demand to actor individual performance, the actor performance must need to satisfy audiences visual leisure enjoyment. So, any global theatres must need have good performance hall and comfortable seats as well as every actor individual excellent performance skill to satisfy any one audience individual visual leisure need in theatre performance market demand and supply view.

How theatre performances and facilities can attract audience individual leisure choice? In may this book , I shall attempt to explain how theatre management strategy implement in order to increase audience number. Readers can learn useful theatre management skills.

Prologue

Table of content

Chapter 1

Past, present and future theater performance development

Chapter 2

What performance skills to future theater performance individual need

Chapter 3

Theater performance brings what social benefit

Chapter 4 Audience choices between theater and cinema movie leisure

PROLOGUE

movie leisure industry p.45-60

1

Past, present and future theater performance Development

● How to improve past theatre performance to be better? Firstly, we need to know whether how our global theatre performance

feature trends. In history of theatre charts , the development of theatre over the past, these performance developed into dramas, how did theatre change over time? As we explore how the theatre has changed over the years. We can see that in some ways the theatre has changed over the years. We can see that in some ways that it did not change that much. A thousand years after the first plays more staged, people still loved bawdy, explicit comedies about society. Later in the restoration period, theatres began to stage so called " machine plays".

What is the history of theatre development ? History of theatre origins of Greek theatre, i.,e. in the levels of the followers of Dionysus, a god of fertility and wine. In the 6th century BC a PRIEST OF Dionysus , by the name of Thespis introduces a new element which can validly be seen as the birth of theatre.

How did Philippine theatre change over the years? After the Japanese occupation, the Philippine theatre has evolved to become an amalgamation of the3 various influences, such that of the Zarzela, comedia, Western classics etc. performances. By the 1950s, theatre had moved out of classrooms and the3 concept of paying for a ticket to see a theatrical performance emerged.

● What are the three origins of theatre development ?

The theatre of ancient Greece consisted of three types of drama:

Tragedy, comedy and Satyr play. The origins of theatre in ancient Greece , according to Arisotle (384 B322 BCE), theatre , are to be found in the festivals. Hence, our nowadays theatre performance is the evolution of modern theatrical production , we take a look at how the theatre has evolved over the year. In the past, theatre had been a welcome distraction. Trim tragedy, comedy, and satyr play performance mainly. In many locations, theatre as performance evolved from other ideas, such as old Roman philosopher , statue. Traditional theatre performance had been developed to today's digital performances in past forms of theatrical technology, due to theatre performance audience visual leisure needs (demand) had been changing.

● What makes a good theatre performance?

Today, theatre performance had been influenced by audience visual leisure changing need. A great theatre performance is one where the characters are compelling . The characters will be the most recognized part of the theatre performance. They arte the people that act out the pitot and deal with the conflict and problems of the plot. The audience will mostly be interested in learning more about the character.

What is a performance in theatre? In performing, acts, a performance generally comprises , an event in which a performer, or group of performers, present one or more works of act to an audience. In instrumental music and drama , a performance is typically described as a " play" . A performance also describes the way in which an actor performs.

What is modern theatre feature? Modern theatre also known as 20th century theatre, impacting Asian, European and American theatre forms. It focused on a board perception of looking in to art, including theatre, critically, e.g. realism, musical theatre, opera are forms on new theatres.

Thus, theatre for development is a type of community-based or it is very important for actors and organizers of the performance or performance project. For example, theatre for positive youth development, theatre teacher needs to educate students how they see performance, which can bring positive social emotional to feel whether the theatre to let audiences to know. So, nowadays, theatre performance is needed to develop through drama. Theatre performance needs to provide visual leisure and education both aims, e.g. theatre actors and performance producers need to learn how to produce and inspire exciting and imaginative theatre, they aim to learn how to provide professional theatre performance production, education and training and visual leisure act performance development aspects, during the performance , the audience was asked what the actors reflected present community concerns and attitudes. A lot of work goes into creating a theatre performance. Today, theatres can generally be divided into two types: Producing theatres or leisure theatres. Producing theatres have creative teams which develop new productions from existing or new work, otherwise, leisure theatre aims to produce any kinds of visual leisure performance aim.

● Future theatre performance ought how to develop?

Future theatre performance tends on technology, scenographic performance, communal argument reality and the future of theatre and performance development and proposed how these might influence and benefit the development of theatre acts and lives, dramatic performance ,e.g. live performance theatres., they will continue to develop on appreciation for in-person experiences.

In the last few years, technological development likes virtual reality theatre and performance will be developed in their own visual leisure unique performance features to let audiences feel the different visual leisure enjoyment by technology performance improvement, e.g. smaller theatres can benefit from a wide range of societal theatres and develop it themselves . Also, in Western country, US , it tends to develop professional non-for-profit theatre field. In development a child's ability to understand the lives of others and fostering a deepe3r sense of compassion. Moreover, the future theatre artistic voice through the experience of live performance.

● How does technology transfer stage performance?

Other kind of future theatre performance development is digital development in theatre. In theatre om audiences ,which will use their experience in theatre and performance on the digital music performance and video performance theatres both aspects. Future theatre industry will be experimenting digital performance. The future of theatre and stage performance is setting up digital kind of leisure performance, it may include: Venue planning, auditorium, seating design, digital performance production, specialist architectural lighting and performance sound, digital platform for the acts. If you are an individual audience customer, you will be influenced to choose to see digital theatre performance more than traditional tool to provide the act students with an in depth view of performances of essential. Rather than considering the real time or temporality of events, digital theatre concerns the interactions of people (audience and actors) sharing the same physical space (in an least one location, if multiple audiences exists).

The first digital theatre is founded in 2009, digital theatre is already the world's leading educational the world's leading educational platform for the performing acts. Today, digital theatres can provide 3 million students in over 2000 schools, colleges and universities across 65 counties with unlimited access to over 1,000 more full length productions and educational resources. However, digital theatre has provided free access to its archive of performances, it had been announced by their accounts managers.

IN the future, any one can watch digital theatre, we can watch digital performance on TV, desktop, tablet and mobile. Screen mirroring via a chromecast dongle from audience mobile or laptop. So, digital theatre can provide any audiences to watch performances in any places. It is a " live" performance placing at least some performers in the same shared physical space with an audience. Hence, digital theatre enriches and enhances the experience of watching a performance with exclusive . So, digital performances have the potential to open up access to the theatre to much wider population, when COVID 19 disease impacts theatres can nor permit open to let many people sit together in theatres. So, virtual performances can help theatres to keep functioning in lockdown or when outdoor performance. So , theatre and performance in digital culture examines the recent history of advanced technologies, including new performance leisure digital media. It will be accepted to watch an performance from desktop , laptop, mobile etc. technological performance platforms in the world.

2

What performance skills to future theater performance individual need

❦

● What are theatrical skills?
The performing arts primarily focus on dance, drama, music and theatre. This means there's often overlap with the film. However, the skills that performer needs to be a performance artist. They may include: confidence, the ability to network and market the performer himself/ herself , self -discipline, on analytical mind the ability to self-reflect, flexibility , teamwork , organization and the management personal characteristics.
To develop a range of physical skills and techniques, e.g. movement, body language , posture, feature, coordination, timing, control, facial expression, eye contract, listening, expression of mood, awareness, interaction with other performers, dance and choral movement. Thus,

performance skills are goal directed actions that a person enacts when performing a task. Focusing on performance skill is what makes occupational therapy's contribution to unique and powerful . Thus, making a good theatre performance , a great theatre performance is one where the characters one compelling. The characters will be the recognized part of the theatre performance. They are the people that act the plot and deal with the conflicts of and problems of the pilot. Also talent and technology is the most important skill to influence any one performer whose theatre music , dance, stage entertainment.

What are some life skills that are used I theatre? Life skills learned in theatre may include : Oral communication skills, creative problem solving abilities, motivation and commitment, willing to work cooperatively, the ability to work independently, time-budget skill. So, it implies that performer individual needs to learn right life skill and like attitude in order to achieve the excellent performances. Theatre performance ought have relationship to any one performer life experience. So., life experience is also one important factor to influence any one theatre performer's performance can bring more attractive or not to satisfy any audience's leisure need. Moreover, another kind acting skills are also important to influence theatre performance. Acting involves a board range of skills, including a well-developed imagination, of speech and the ability to interpret drama.

Another kind acting skills are also important factor to influence any one theatre performer's performance can bring more attration or not to satisfy any audience 's leisure need. Moreover, acting involves a board range of skills, including a well developed imagination, emotional facility , physical expressivity, vocal projection , kind clarity of speech and the ability to inteerpret drama, another kind is performance skills, performance skills are goal-directed actions that a person enacts when performing a task. It causes on performance skill is what makes occupational therapy's contribution to unique and powerful.

● main elements influences theatre performance

Thus, to achieve the best theatre performance objective, the three basic elements of theatre may include : performers, audience , director, theatre space, design aspects (scenery, costume, lighting and sound), text which includes focus purpose point of view. However, the most important life skill , any one performer needs to learn in theatre is communication. Many theatre performers develop the ability to speak clearly, incidly and thoughtfully . When the performer acts on stage , he is comfortable speaking to range groups of people. Many theatre companies look for this in an individual when individuals who can demonstrate excellent verbal and written communication skills, teamwork, and attraction performing actions in order to satisfy audience leisure need, when they decide to buy ticket to see the theatre performance show.

Thus, when a theatre student hopes to learn theatre skills easily or understands easily. He/she ought have these psychologicall attitufes: Self awarenesses, being open and receptive to criticism, teamwork, time management, dealing with all types of different people, confidence and public speaking skills, being realistic. He also needs to know whether he ought how to learn theatre acting, such as learn to use masterclass, read actor biographies or autobiographics, be more abservant of people in action, listen to podcasts, teach others, study people who are like what skills the perfrmer can learn from drama. Drama promotes communicataion skills, teamwork,dialogue, negotiation, socialization. It stimulates th imagination and creativity. It also develops a better understanding of human behavior and empathy with situations that might seem distant. Performance skills in drama may include: movement-soft, gentle, heavy light , quick show, resture signals with your hands/arms to show feelings, facial expressions wide eyed, norrow eyed, raised eyebrows, troubled permanent frown, down turned mouth, eye contact staring, glaring fleeting, voice-pitch high and squeaky , low and soft etc. body language skills.

In fact, students involved in drama performanc coursework when one student decides to learn theatre performance or experience outscored non-act students. Drama can improve skills and academic performance in children and youth with learning disabilities . Because the practical role performing acts plays in a well-rounded. It's about learning transferable life skills. By observing others students learn to make creative choices on stage by creativity and imagination. So, Drama classes can give performance chance to let theatre students to attempt to improve their performing skills. Also, drama enhances students' artistic and creative abilities and gives them a better performance improvement through learning which involves thought, feeling and action, workshops and attendance at theatre performances.

On conclusion, the performing acts primarily focus on dance, drama, music and theatre performforming acts students can develop skills needed for life and music, theatre, and speech and debate activities are ideas for them to learn through intensive research not just facts and every time performance learning courts can let they have performance practice experience to improve their next performance more attractive. Hence, every time theatre performance practice can help any theatre students to improve thwir life skills, acting skills , performance skills absolutely.

3

Theater performance brings what social benefit

● Why do our society need theatre performance?
What benefits of music, drama, dance, act performance , they can bring benefits to our society? How they can impact our social future development? What negative impacts, they will influence to our social development? I shall attempt to answer these questions concern future theatre performance whether it ought continue to develop or not.
Theatre can improve social bonding, allow do emotions to be explored in a safe space, develop the emotional and cognitive skills to deal with a complicated world, and kick-start coversations about important issues. How does theatre contribute to society? The theatre , dance and other performing arts can teach people how to express themselves effectively and can also be a tool though with people with disabilities can communicate. In addition to teaching self-expression, the performing arts, help society or a whole in self-knowledge and understanding.
What is the purpose of theatre for social change? It is unlike other kind of theatre, theatre for social change is a

performance to raise awareness about the impact of social issues through community engagement process. How does theatre have an economic impact on society? Theatre and performing arts are also hugely imported to economies and brings societies positive impact. The US Bureau of economic analysis showed that 3.2 % of US GDP around US$504 billions is attributable to arts and culture (compared with the entire US travel and tourism industry, which accounts for 2.8% of GDP).

Hence, in theatre performance, originally a supplemental performance by an actor or actress, who kept all or past of the theatre performance. The benefits of drama performance, the benefits are physical , emotional , social and they help to develop , health society in many cases the quality of any performance reliance on an performance.

● Threatre performance brings what beneftis to impact our future social development ?

some benefits include emotional, social , physical and even academic aspects, instead of economyic benefit to societies. What are theatre performance emotional benefit? On student theatre performance educstional aspect, a range of emotions and encourage them to understand and deal with similar feelings . They may be experiencing, aggession and tension are releases in a sage , controlled theatre performance learning environment. So, there are five benefits to students who participate in theatre arts. They may include: helping them to build empathy emotion, whe kids participate any characters playing in thetre performance. They can learn how to control emotions to keep calm more than engry feeling or emotions in any future working environment easily when they need to work in society.

Improvement academic performance, participation in drama boosts students feelings of belonging and keeps them motivated at school, building goal-setting direction mind, self-esteem. All of these positive emotions, any student may be influenced when he/she can spend time to participate any kinds of theatre performance learning chance. So, the main purpose of theatre performances i s that , in fact, the purpose of theatre is to provide through job to people. The threatre is a branch of the performing arts and it is concerned with the acting our stories in front of the audience. The benefits of performing arts include improving life skills and academic performance to students.

● How can watching theatre benefit the mind?

These who watch live theatre have a reduction of stress and tension. The experience is to immersive that the audience can quickly become in the show. Live theatre allows you to forget about your daily stresses and feel as peace when you are watching in theatre hall. Hence, the benefits of drama for children, a good understand of characters, roles and subtext of plays will allow childrens' emotional intelligence building through the use of imagination, also live performance could also provide a host of developmental benefits, including improved emotionable child,individual can also bring emotional intelligence from theatre art performance learning, it focuses students can spend how much time to participate in youth theatre and still loves to attend live performances.

What re theatre performance social benefits? community theatres involves more participants, present more performances of more. Participation in community theatre brings with it on immediate social circle, and all the networking benefits. How does theatre contribute to society? The theatre, dance and music and drama etc.performance acts can teach people to express themselves effectively, and can also be a tool through which people with disabilities can communicate . In addition to teaching self-expression, the performing arts help society as a whole in self-knowledge and understanding can theatre bring positive and/or negative social change?

Theatre for social change is one of many frameworks that can be used to solve problems and create changes in society. However, the unique part of the theatre , which utilize and engage directly with the full human body. Horeover, theatre performance can let many studetns feel that theatre helps them develop the confidence that's essential to speaking clearly, lucidly and throughfully. Acting onstage teaches students how to be comfortable speaking in front of large audiences, and some of student theate performing learn classes will give them additional experience telling to groups.

● What physical benefits can bring to individual from theatre performance?

Instead of theatre performance can bring social, economic emotion benefits to society , student individual emotion, economic income growth. Whether theatre performance can bring benefits to audiences when they buy ticket to watch any kinds of theatre performance in theatres. How can watching theatre benefit the audience individual mind? Theatre encourages and expresses emotions in their most extreme form. As a human, watching any kinds of theatre performance or listening any kinds of music performance in theatre, others express emotions can trigger that their emotion repsonse in audience individual feeing as well. Theatre shows healthy to let any one audience to feel all types of emotin and to understand empathy. So, it seems that theatre is not only entertaining, but also has both mental and physical health benefits crucial for a healthy lifestyle. When audiences who attend performing arts events are healthier, have lower anxiety, and are less likely to suffer from depression.

● Can theatre performance improve studend individual academic performance?

Can student often watch theatre performance to improve his/her academic performance? It seems that these questions concern whether watching theatre performance, which can boost academic performance. It shows that educational psychologists believe that engaging with performing arts can boost the academic performance of the average child by 4 % when drama is part of curriculum.

The social benefits of theatre and performance include better self-efficiency in children and teenagers, as well as making them better equipped to broach complex subjects. How does theatre help education? Using drama and theatre as a tool to teach is not only effective, it will also bring the necessary change in the learning process for students. This concept helps students learn better, instead of simply being observers. They get to be a part of the learning process. So, theatre can enrich, student individual life, because these it does not harm, expresses a basic human instinct, brings people together models democratic discourse, contributes to education and literary , sparks economic revitalization, and influences how we think and feel generation's learning life.

● How do the arts improve academic performance?

Student s that like a combination of arts programs demonstrate improved verbal, reading, and math skills, and also show a greater capacity for higher ordered thinking skills, such as analyzing and problem solving. How can theatre help student learning development in his/her learning living experience? Many students find that theatre helps them develop the confidence that is essential to speaking clearly and thoughfully. Acting on stage teaches student how to be comfortable speaking in front of large audiences, and some of students their theatre classes will give them additional experience talking to groups. The recent university university research explored the educational and social benefits from theatres, theatres can improve social bonding, allow for emotions to be explored in a hallpy life environment. So, students can improve their communication skills and their capacity to read -write and speak when they can attempt to spend some extra time to participate to learn theatre performance in schools.

I means that little time spending theatre performance learning participation , it can improve student individual academic performance in possible , other excess time spending theatre performance learning participation it can not improve student individual academic learning performance, even it can bring worse academic result, because busy theatre students, involved in a production or other theatre projects when also taking a heavy academic load. So, I believe that theatre performance learning participation ought improve any student individual academic performance, but it depends on whether he/she spends some extra little time to particpate any kinds of theatre learning performance or spends more time t participate any kinds of theatre learning performance. It is value research whether theatre performance how to influence academic performance on education issue aspect.

4

Audience choices between theater and cinema movie leisure

---♡---

● Supply and demand view to future theatre and cinema movie leisure industry

In audience behavioral leisure psychology view, when the audience consumer has time to spend watching lesiure activity. When he feels leisure time is less , he will make watching lesiure either he makes purcahse ticket decision to enter cinema to watch movie or he makes purchase ticket decision to enter theatre to watch art performance, So, it seems that any kinds of movie may be any kinds of art performance competitors. Howwver, those factors may influence theatre performance audience number, they may include whether that art performance is attractive to satisfy audience's visual leisure feelingl, how many movies number is supplied to cinemas or how many art performance number is supplied to theatres, how many audiences number choice to buy ticket to watch art performance or, watch movie.

So, it implies that movie number may influence theatre art performance audiences number because watching leisure audiences may watch any kinds of movies or theatre performances. In supply and demand view , it explains when the consumer feels watching leisure need in any holiday, he needs either to watch the movie or watch the theatre performance. Hence, whether the month has how many movies have already been watched by audiences in cinemas. Their movies number may absolute influence theatre performance audiences choice to watch which movie in order to replace any one theatre performance.

Hence, any one theatre performance provider, whose competitors may include other theatre performance providers and other movie providers both , even online theatre performaners, because any one audience may choose to watch art performance from internet channel. Hence, future theatre performance market competition is serious. I believe that instead of whether the theatre performance arrangement is attractive factor, ticket price is resonable factor, performance time factor, the theatre design facility factor may also influence audiences wathing to the theatre performance choice.

It means that theatre facility environment may be one influential factor to persuade audiences to enter the theatre to watch the art performances. If the theatre facility environment light and sound facilities are not supplied enough to satisfy audience 's listening and watching feeling. They can not sit comfortable in the theatre seats. Any of these external theatre environment facility factor also may influence audiences number to the threatre. So, future theatre environment facilities must be needed to raise quality in order to achieve the high service enjoyable level to satisfy audiences leisure need, e.g. electronic moving seats, they can let audiences have auto rising or fallig feeling when they are still sitting on the seat in theatres. Music must need soft music, it can not permit loud in theatre environment, because soft music can let audiences to feel comfortable to watch and listen any kind of art performance. The art performance time can not perform too short time, e.g. half hour, but performance time can not be long time, e.g. more than two hours, because the art performance time is too short , it will let audiences feel ticket price is too high, but if the art performance time is too long, it will let audiences feel boring when they need spend long time to sit on seats.

Hence, any one art performance time is also one important factor to influence audience individual leisure feeling. Moreover, any kinds of theatre art performance must need have educational aim. It means that the art performers must need to let students feel that they can learn knowledge to be applied to their life experiences after they watched the art performance, because nowadays, many audiences are young, they choose to watch the kind of art performance, they need have leisure feeling and learning new life experience knowledge from the kind of art performance, because some young people choose to watch the kind of art performance, they hope to learn new life experience knowledge in order to pursue art performance career.

So, whether the art performance can let th young student to feel that he can learn art performance skills or not, it will influence the art performance learner to choose to watch the kind of art performance or not. Hence, whether the kind of art performance, it has educational feelingto the art performance learning audience, it will influence whether the art performance learner to choose to go to theatre to watch the art performers; performance in theatre, because if the art performance learners feel the kind of art performance can not let them to feel they can learn any new art performance skill, they won't choose to buy ticket to watch the kind of art performance. So, any one art performance provider must need to consider performance leisure and performance educational both aims in order to satisfy art performance lesiure audiences and art performance learner audiences their psychological needs.

In fact, instead of lesiure art performance audiences, learning art performance, they will be another main audiences source, such as art performance students, because they need to go to classroom to listen art performance teachers to learn any kinds of art performance skill, they also choose to buy ticket to watch any kinds of art performance because watching art performance may be another kind of learning art performance skillful method to raise improve their art performance skills, So , future art performers need to know how to perform in order to satisfy art performance student individual learning need. So,, future any art performance students may be any one art performance service provider 's audiences. They can not neglect this new art performance student audience group in future art performance market development trend.

On conclusion, when art performance students feel the kind of art performance can satisfy their art performance skill learning need. They won't choose spend much time to buy ticket to enter cinemas to watch movies, even if the kind of art performance service leisure provider can provide any kinds of attractive art performance to let audiences to watch, as well as the theatre facilities can be improved more comfortable feeling, then many movie audiences will be persuaded to buy ticket to enter theatres to watch any kinds of art performances.

So, future theatre performance market development success depends on art performer individual performance skill, theatre facilities service improvement, art performance ticket price and performance time factors. Also, the difference between movie performancers and art performancers is that movie performaners can not do "life show". Otherwise, art performancers can do life show, life show is one kind of life experience, every art performer needs to do life experience, perform on theatre, they can have immediate emotion feeling from audiences whether they like their art performance or they dislike their art performance. When they are performing life show in theatre.So, their satisfactory feeling ought be more than movie performers. Moreover, art performance behearsal time ought be more than movie performance rehearsal time, if they hope to perform the most effective result. Hence, art performance market, it still have these strengths to win movie audience individal leisure choice in global art performance theatre market.